"How to
SCREW UP
Your Business
Without Trying And
THE SECRETS TO STOP IT
From Happening"

STEPHAN J. DANIELS

Copyright © 2021 Stephan J. Daniels
All rights reserved.
ISBN

DEDICATION

To Kim, my rock!

CONTENTS

Acknowledgments vii
Introduction ix

1 History Lessons 1
2 Systems 6
3 The Help 12
4 Time Management 18
5 Math 24
6 Philosophies 30
7 Marketing 35
8 Crisis Management 47

About The Author 51

ACKNOWLEDGMENTS

To my parents, job well done. And all my family and friends for their support.

INTRODUCTION

> *"The man to go sailing with is the man who has been shipwrecked."*
> **Daniel DaFoe**

Firstly, I want to start off by saying thank you! Thank you for buying this book and taking some time to educate yourself about what you are trying to do in your life at this moment in time. Thank you for taking a chance to listen to what I have to say about the business of business.

It is my hope that by writing this little book that it will be of great benefit to you in your endeavor. Even if you only acquire one benefit from reading this book, it will be worth the cost. Whether you are starting your own business or if you find yourself to be a "necessity entrepreneur".

I want you to be able to clean away the clutter and foolishness that passes for authority on business that permeates our society today. There is a great deal of information available for you in the world today. However, there is a need for actionable intelligence.

I want you to find in these pages pragmatic insights into how to run your business as a business should be run. With an iron fist! And most importantly to make money!

That's right, I know that profit is a four-letter word these days, but last time I checked, you and I get paid with dollars, not likes or hits or anything else. Dollars. That's it.

Does that sound cold or insensitive? Perhaps, but it's real. I don't play video games, and I don't live in a virtual world; I live in the real world and being in business is about making a profit.

But it's also the truth. I'm not here to spoon feed you any B.S. There are plenty of places to go and get that if you want it. However, this book isn't one of them.

I don't know you on a personal level, but I'm going to assume that your parents raised you well and you have morals and ethics. I would also like to infer that it's going to transfer into your business, as it should.

However, that doesn't distract from the fact that the power company gets paid dollars as well, and if you neglect to pay them, off goes the lights. If nothing else, this book is, at the very least, pragmatic. In its pages you will find little nuggets that may be worth gold to you. Pick what you like and dispose of what you don't. That is what I hope it to be. Your blueprint for profit. The best of luck to you!

1 History Lessons

> *"We are not makers of history.*
> *We are made by history"*
> **Martin Luther King**

First, we need to start out with a little history lesson. I need to give you some background information so that you have an idea of where I came from and what on earth gives me the authority, or the audacity to write a book about business!

My professional background is in the restaurant business; I'll touch base on that a bit more in later chapters. For the majority of my adult working life, I've been immersed in this field. The journey began back in 1980 when my brothers decided to go into business for themselves. My brother John had worked in several restaurants since graduating from high school and decided he wanted to venture out on his own at the ripe old age of twenty. With $3,000 in working capital, he and my brother Chris established a catering venture in a small, rented space for $150 a month. All of this accomplished while still working other jobs.

I know what you're thinking, "$150 a month for rent?" It was 1980 and prices reflect that era, so it's all relative.

However, $3000 was a substantial amount of money in those days, just as the rent was. Also, if you dream of opening your own restaurant, bear in mind that my brothers purchased all used equipment, and let me tell you, it was already old by 1980 standards. Interestingly, I think we still have some of it to this day. The takeaway here is: prioritize cash flow and don't buy brand new if you can help it. Cash flow is more important than your mother.

The importance of cash flow is not just reserved for the restaurant business, but all types of businesses. It is a fundamental principle that should never be overlooked. And no offense to your mother.

As I said, he continued working at his other job to maintain cash flow until they could get the catering business off the ground. He did this for some time as the catering business had its ups and downs. Then, one day, a friend of his suggested he start selling sandwiches. So, guess what? He seized the opportunity and opened a small storefront that sold sandwiches.

In other words, he adapted and evolved. He had to. This book is meant to be about learning. Hopefully, you will glean insights from the multitude of mistakes we made building a business from scratch. And let me tell you, we made a bunch. A crucial lesson: don't get to stuck on a single idea when starting a business. Sometimes you must let go and allow something better to emerge. It's counterintuitive for sure, but such is life.

It is at about this time that I joined the family business as a young man, juggling part time while still in high school. I often joke that the first time I went to a restaurant was when I started to work in one. Our clientele gradually grew as word of mouth spread about our little restaurant.

1 HISTORY LESSONS

Believe it or not, we still have customers that to this day, order food from us. Not many, but a few. That's the lifelong value of a customer which I will touch base on in later chapters. Now, that is worth repeating. WE STILL HAVE CUSTOMERS from 1980. I hope you got that, and I didn't mean to yell because it's important to know what the lifetime or long-term value of a customer or LCV is. I will touch on that more later as well. If you went to business school and never heard of this, you got screwed!

After spending several years in our initial location, we made the strategic decision to move to a free-standing building that we purchased. This was a smart move on the part of my brothers because they used funds from the business to invest in an asset that typically appreciates over time, though not always guaranteed.

It's rare to stumble upon a deal like ours if you're thinking of opening a restaurant and very likely you will find that you will have to rent. In this case, it would be prudent to try and find a location that was previously a restaurant and already meets all the necessary codes and regulations. This way, you can avoid significant capital expenditures, particularly on essential items like a grease trap, which can cost a fortune. I realize that this sounds blunt, but it is the reality of the industry, especially considering the high failure rates among restaurants. At the end of the day, business is still business.

Incidentally, I aim to sprinkle this book with little jewels like the one just mentioned. I may be redundant at times, but there is good reason: to ensure you avoid costly mistakes as you are trying not to screw up your business. So it is worth repeating and important to pay attention to the little jewels – they're here for your benefit.

After a few years in this location (which is still our flagship store), my brothers decided to expand into a larger location in another town. We opted to rent a former pizzeria which had much of the necessary build out already in place. Like I said earlier, this make sense. We had to clean it up and get some used equipment to get started. This location was in a strip mall which was owned by a man who was very fair in his dealings. As a word of caution, this will not always be the case in business dealings. As they say, you will oftentimes find yourself swimming with the sharks out there.

We were presented with a rent-to-own option which we did not exercise at the time – a decision that was a mistake! We should have purchased the building and rented it out. By doing so, we could have paid for the real estate out of the business revenue. Even if the restaurant didn't thrive, we would have still owned the real estate, a valuable asset. It was another lesson learned: indeed hindsight is 20/20.

Again, I'm sharing insights from a restaurant owners' perspective, as well as that of an entrepreneur. Your goal is to maximize the wealth generated from your enterprise. Yes, it would be admirable to aspire to save endangered species like snow leopards along the way, but let's not forget the fundamental purpose of businesses: to generate profits. Ultimately, your goal is to create a lifestyle that aligns with your desires, free from the dictates of others. To achieve this, you must be willing to do the things you need to do now, so you can secure a lifetime of freedom.

When I hear people talk about security, my stomach turns. Look around you – there is very little that is truly secure, especially now! As the old saying goes, death and taxes are the only certainties in life; everything else is uncertain. Therefore,

1 HISTORY LESSONS

focus your efforts to work ON your business and not IN it! That is a critical distinction, and I urge you to pay attention to that. If you neglect this crucial aspect, you're going to be running around putting out fires and dealing with endless minor crises. If you want to do that, consider getting a job as a fireman. It's critical to get real as to what you are about to embark upon before you even sign a rental lease. Frankly, this is where the wheels started to come off in our business. We grew too rapidly and lost sight of the fundamentals and got careless. We failed to establish proper systems and the consequences were profound – the price paid for our oversight was blood, sweat, and plenty of tears.

In our defense, we were young and much of what we did was trial by fire. But hey, maybe that's why you're reading this book --to avoid making the same mistakes, am I right? I have faith in your intelligence and your commitment to do your homework. And by learning from my battle stories, so you will be better equipped to succeed and live the life you truly desire!

You may already be aware of the daunting statistics surrounding small business failure rate in the United States – around 90 percent in the first year, and for restaurants, it is approximately 60 percent. The odds are not in your favor before you even open the doors. But I'm not here to dampen your spirits or discourage you; I'm simply presenting you with some facts to go on. You can easily get caught up in over-analyzing every detail but try not to fall prey to it. Sooner or later, you must pull the trigger and take action. And yes, you will make mistakes – it is inevitable! The key is to do it fast and get it out of the way. But most importantly, learn from the mistakes, and move forward without dwelling on them! That is the essential takeaway.

2 Systems

> *"A bad system will beat a good person every time"*
> **W. E Deming**

One of the first classes I had in college was a class called Introduction to Systems Thinking. It was developed at M.I.T in the electrical engineering department by Jay Forrester's research on industrial dynamics way back in the 1960s. I will be honest with you; it wasn't easy for me to grasp. I have never considered myself academic by any means. Interestingly, M.I.T. developed a game called the "beer game" to teach students the fundamentals of systems thinking. I thought, *naively*, "I love beer, so this should be easy!" Well as it turns out, it's not. In fact, it's quite complex.

The "beer game" utilizes a beer distributorship business model to demonstrate concepts such as the ebb and flow of products, in this case beer, and the time lapses inherent within the various funnels of the system. Think about yourself for a moment. You are a human being – at least I hope you are. Look at how many systems you have within your own body: the respiratory system, central nervous, cardiovascular system, and so forth These systems all work in concert to regulate body temperature, breathing, blood pressure and so on. These are extraordinarily complex systems within systems. When one component breaks down, it triggers a ripple effect on all the others within the network. Now look at the world around you. Just as your body is comprised of intricate systems, so too does the world. There are political systems, economic systems, and environmental systems – each are equally as complex and interconnected as those of the human body. We find ourselves integrated within them and influenced by their dynamics.

Now, I'm not saying you should run out and pursue a PhD in systems thinking. What I am saying is that having the proper systems in place when you launch a business will be of immense help to you. Perfection is unattainable – such is the nature of life on Earth. However, dedicating some thought to your systems before you start will give you a significant edge over your competition. The ability to step back from your business and analyze how your integrated systems are functioning is a skill that few possess. This underscores the recurring theme of this book: focus your efforts to work on your business, not in it.

It's important to recognize that these systems interact with one another, and sometimes, that interaction is not a good thing.

Let's take a brief look at perhaps one of the most important systems any enterprise can have: human resources. Whether you're the only person working in the business or have a small team, if you want to expand, sooner or later you will have to hire other human beings.

While there has been much talk about how robots will replace humans in the workforce, and that is true to some extent, it is important to recognize that we humans are here to stay. Yeah humans! Therefore, it's a prudent idea to seek out, hire, and train the best talent you can find. On the flip side, it's equally important to be willing to let individuals go when need be. A wise man long ago told me to hire slowly, and fire quickly. I wish I had listened to him sooner. It could have saved a significant amount of time, money, and heartache.

I won't delve into politics, but I believe in the capitalist system as well as the entrepreneurial spirit that thrives in this country. With that said, there is one area within your business, especially in the early stages, where you must be unwavering: personnel management Your profitability hinges on it. If there is one thing that can infect an entire company, it's a single bad employee. They are like cancer that can metastasis throughout the entire business organism. I've seen it happen firsthand! Don't hesitate to address the issue and show them the door. If handling underperforming employees is not your forte, quickly delegate it to someone else. However, as the business owner, you are ultimately responsible for human resources management and may have to do it on your own. It's crucial to handle these situations professionally, that goes without saying. Sometimes tough decisions need to be made and actions taken for the health of your business.

These employees reflect your business and are part of that system. Oftentimes, the most significant part of your system. Strive to hire the best possible individual, although this is becoming more challenging by the day. Unfortunately, there is a growing number of humans who feel the world owes them something, viewing employment as a favor to you by merely showing up to work. In reality, it's quite the opposite. If you find yourself in this situation, do yourself a favor and show them the door! The quicker the better. The world owes us nothing – not a job, not a college education, nothing. However, it does give us all one invaluable thing: opportunity.

Allow me give you a quick example. Some friends and I were golfing one day. Around the fifth hole, a gentleman who was golfing alone came up on us. Following golf etiquette, we allowed him to play through so as not to slow him down. As he approached the tee, we were all struck by the same amazing observation: this guy had only one arm. Yet, as he teed off with a powerful swing, he crushed it! I mean crushed it a long drive right down the center of the fairway. We had eight arms between us and none of us could not tee off that well. This experience serves as a powerful reminder, as I said, the world owes us nothing. This remarkable guy refused to feel sorry for himself. He overcame a physical limitation, embraced his circumstance and focused his mind on what he could do and did it! This is a profound distinction worth remembering.

In thinking in terms of your business systems, try to leverage your mind rather than your body. There is no reason to reinvent the wheel. Instead, seek out and adopt good ideas and eventually, you can customize them to fit your unique needs. Take Henry Ford, for example. He did not invent the production line; he adopted the idea from the efficient processes and systems used in meat-packing plants in Chicago. He saw how each man had a particular role and responsibility and that was all they did. By reverse-engineering the production line from disassembly, same as in the slaughterhouse, to assembly in Model T Fords, he revolutionized manufacturing. You have the same opportunity to embrace the practice of learning from others and adapting proven strategies to suit your business. In fact, I strongly encourage it.

It's crucial for your employees to receive clear directives outlining their responsibilities and expected outcomes – essentially, instill discipline within your organization. To borrow from the military, maintain a clear chain of command and avoid fraternizing with the troops. They must understand that you are the leader. The human resource system serves as the hardware of your business, perhaps the most important component alongside the accounting system for monitoring cash flow, and the marketing system for generating revenue. They are all important. The more you can learn about systems before starting your business, the better prepared you will be for success.

For example, as someone in the restaurant business, I am meticulous about checking every time my staff fills salad dressings and discards the container. Why? Because many times they leave a significant amount of product in the container then toss it into the trash. To me, that's money, my money, they are tossing into the trash. This adds up quickly in terms of waste. If I had a dime for every time I caught this, I'd be wealthier. The point is, with proper systems in place, you can effectively fend off costly waste and retain more cash. Properly established systems should almost operate like autopilot. Truthfully, many employees just don't seem to care beyond collecting their paycheck and seem to be just putting their time. Without effective systems to mitigate this type of activity, profits quickly vanish.

2 SYSTEMS

    I don't mean to come across as cynical, but that is the reality of how the world works and behaves. You don't have to believe me. However, you're going to find out quickly that I'm onto something. It is essential to hold everyone in your organization accountable and lead by example. With robust systems in place from the start, you'll significantly reduce your stress level.

3 THE HELP

> *"The employer generally gets the employee he deserves"*
> **J Paul Getty**

I am sure that you have heard of Pareto's Law, or the 20/80 rule, as it is more commonly called. It is a principle that is applicable in all aspects of your life. I will be discussing it in the context of your workforce. Simply put, 20% of your employees will contribute to 80% of the work. Let that sink in for a moment. I'll repeat it just so it sinks in. 20% of your employees will contribute to 80% of the work. Still not convinced? Try this experiment: over the next week, look in your closet and pay attention to which clothes you wear most frequently. You will find that you likely wear just 20% of your clothes and the other 80% will just hang there untouched, perhaps even feeling a bit jealous of their frequently worn counterparts.

Go ahead and give it a try and see if I'm wrong. Spoiler alert: I'm not. While sometimes the ratio may vary slightly, on average it tends to come in at 20/80. Your staff are not much different from the clothes in your closet, in a manner of speaking.

3 THE HELP

Now, I'm no human resource expert, but I've had the privilege of working with thousands of individuals throughout the years. Honestly, if most of them approached me on the street, I probably would not remember them. Only a handful truly stand out as exceptional. Given the nature of my business, age often played a role, but even then, I could discern the top performers from the rest.

The same dynamic will likely play out within your team. You will have some truly outstanding players who really want to be successful and will be productive contributors. However, the majority – the other 80% – will simply be riding on the coattails of these top performers. In my experience, most employees don't share the same level of dedication and commitment as business owners do. They often lack the same sense of urgency and may not fully grasp the gravity of keeping the business afloat. When you're losing sleep at night concerned about making payroll, keeping the doors open and the lights on, they're thinking about what's important in their own lives – taking kids to softball practice or making fantasy football picks. This misalignment of priorities is a common challenge faced by business owners, and it's essential to recognize and address it proactively.

It's a common scenario: your employees received their paycheck every two weeks while you're grappling with the challenges of running a business and ensuring its survival. I used to think that this only happened to me. And rest assured, it won't be unique to you either. It is a shared experience among many business owners. If you ever find yourself in a like-minded group of fellow business owners, you will discover that it's a common issue. Now, I want to be quite clear: not all employees fit this description. There are certainly hardworking and dedicated individuals out there. However, remember Pareto's law. Just as 20% of your employees may contribute to 80% of the work, a similar distribution may exist when it comes to work ethic and dedication. I engage with individuals from various industries, businesses that are very different from my own, and regardless the sector, stories are in abundance of employee's questionable work ethic or lack thereof. This issue can quickly spread and become a cancer within your organization if not addressed promptly and effectively.

As a rule of thumb, by the time you turn eleven years old, your foundation has been laid, so to speak. Translation: your upbringing plays a significant role in shaping your work ethic and values. I won't dwell too much on this topic, but it's worth noting that a good work ethic comes from the home. Fortunately, my father made sure I knew this at an early age. I had chores every day, and guess what? I never received payment for them. Nowadays, such an approach might be considered harsh, but in reality, it's simply preparing children for the realities of life – a valuable lesson.

"The children of today love luxury, they show disrespect of their elders." – Socrates This sentiment underscores the importance of instilling a strong work ethic and respect for others from a young age.

Once again, it's important to emphasize that you don't have to be a jerk. However, you do have to be firm in your expectations. This might require some practice on your part, but with time, you will become more adept at asserting yourself and maintaining a diplomatic demeanor. Consider implementing the three strikes rule, and make sure that your employees are aware of it from the onset. This way, there is no chance for back-peddling on their part. In large corporations with layers of management, it's called being "written up", a "performance warning", or similar terms.

It's important to remember, as a small business owner, you're not likely structured as the large corporations just yet. Therefore, clearly communicate your expectations verbally to your employees. If you consider creating an employee manual, do so with the understanding that employees may not take the time to read it thoroughly I find that verbalization, accompanied by eye contact, fosters better engagement and understanding. While it's true that many problematic employees may weed themselves out over time, not all will. That's why it's crucial that you address any issues, and if necessary, show them the door quickly. This will free up your time to focus on recruiting the right candidate who aligns with your business goals.

I want to emphasize that labor costs will likely be the most significant expense in your business. Your employees are indeed an expense. I'm not trying to be cold but when you review your balance sheet at the end of every month, pay close attention to the bottom of the sheet to see if you earned a profit. I'm no accountant, but if you see red around those numbers, it indicates that you've lost money. As you scan the rest of the balance sheet, the one number that will likely stand out prominently will be labor costs. Therefore, managing these costs effectively is crucial for maintaining profitability in your business.

Why do you think that large companies lay off thousands of employees during economic downturns? Expense, expense, expense. They streamline operations and reduce expenses to maintain profitability. They make do with what they have.

Investing in machine automation technologies, such as robots, becomes attractive options as they can often be depreciated, perform tasks more efficiently and consistently, and machines don't require sick leave or benefits. Large corporations are investing in machines that are now making hamburgers and pizza.

The mindset of business is to maximize profit ethically, and this often involves closely evaluating the return on investment (ROI) of staff.

TIP:
"What gets measured improves."

It's worth emphasizing, even if it is redundant, that when you carefully analyze your finances, which you absolutely should, you'll realize that the staff is the most significant expense you will have likely have in your business. From wages and benefits to vacation pay and various government-mandated costs, it's a small fortune. Therefore, whatever that number turns out to be, it is imperative that each staff member generates value that exceeds these costs as much as possible. You may be wondering if that number is 5%, 10%, or 13%? The specific target may vary depending on your industry and business model, but clearly, the higher, the better. Ultimately the goal is to maximize your bottom line, your profit margin, and your bank balance. That's why I'm an advocate for a focus on productivity, both for yourself and your staff. It's all about GSD... get stuff done.

3 THE HELP

Steve's reminder:
What's the #1 reason why you got into business? To build wealth!

I understand that this perspective may be controversial, but why would you pay the janitor as much as your top salesperson? That does not seem to make good business sense. This may only makes sense to the bureaucrat who came up with the lame idea in the first place. In essence, it should be about aligning compensation with value creation. Salespeople play a critical role in generating revenue, and their compensation is often tied to their performance. If the salespeople are not bringing in sales, then there would be no revenue to sustain the business. Accounting would have nothing to count. And the janitor would have nothing to clean when your unable to sustain covering the rent. All because you have no sales. Pretty bleak, but while fairness is a noble ideal, the harsh truth is that life and business aren't always fair. Don't be seduced by bright shiny things because business is still business. This may mean compensating high-performing employees, such as salespeople, more generously than others. Speaking of value creation...

Hint: Don't ever take an employees' loyalty for granted. Praise them and reward them. Employees who feel valued and appreciated are more likely to remain committed and engaged, contributing to the overall success of your business. When a loyal employee stops caring, it's a warning sign that should not be ignored and could ultimately impact productivity and morale... then your business is in trouble!

4 Time Management

"Time is the most important coin in your life."
— **Carl Sandburg**

It's essential to slay the *"time vampires"* in your life and your business. That's right, use the silver nail right in the heart. You see, these are individuals who have no compunction about wasting their own time and will think nothing at all about wasting yours. Don't let them drain your precious time and productivity. They, the time vampires, come to you at all hours with questions or requests that they could have easily addressed themselves if they'd just put forth a bit of effort.

It's crucial to organize your time effectively to maximize productivity and minimize disruption as much as possible. Research suggests that on average, a person is interrupted every three minutes, and it takes approximately half an hour to regain focus and productivity. I'm not going to reference that statistic but it's pretty accurate. The ability to maintain laser-like focus is critical to desired outcomes. While you shouldn't rely solely on my word, I encourage you to research the evidence to learn even more about the importance of time management.

4 TIME MANAGEMENT

With the onslaught of the digital age where various forms of media are at our fingertips vying for your attention, it becomes even more important to able to focus on the task at hand. You must recognize that it will not only be others who will attempt to steal your time, but that you will also need to self-regulate your own time wisely. I'm guilty of this myself. It starts out innocently enough. You're online looking for a particular item and the next thing you know you're watching home movies of someone's dog surfing or reading an opinion on climate change. It happens, I get it. The point is DON'T FALL FOR IT! Remember the eleventh commandment...

"Manage thy time."

I have heard of some people who opt to communicate solely via fax machine. Why? It is a deliberate strategy to force you to slow down and carefully consider the message you are about to send.

You absolutely must be willing to slay these time vampires. It will not be easy, but it must be done. This is not only crucial for maintaining productivity, but it is also a matter of respect as well. When individuals fail to respect their own time, how will they respect yours? They likely won't. Therefore, it's essential to set firm boundaries and assertively communicate expectations regarding your time. Be firm! It's ok. If you want to be liked, get a dog.

Those interruptions and the time it requires to get refocused can cost significantly more in terms of productivity. Lee Iacocca, the former chairman of Chrysler Motors, was once asked how much productive time he had during his day. His candid reply, "About forty-five minutes." That's not much during the average day and underscores the importance of minimizing distractions and optimizing focus to make the most of your limited time. You must dictate your terms of engagement.

For example, when faced with interruptions like "Walter" who knocks on your door just as you are about to produce your opus and says the classic, "Hey, do have a minute?" Don't even think about it. Put a fork in this one A.S.A.P. You could pull out a stopwatch, click it and say, "go." However, that is not a very diplomatic approach. An alternative approach would be to clearly communicate your availability and priorities while maintaining professionalism and respect. Perhaps something like, "Walter, right now I don't have a minute as I'm finishing a detailed project, but later today at 2 p.m. we could take more than a minute to talk. Does that work for you?" By connecting visually, communicating clearly, and proposing an alternative time, you demonstrate respect for both your own time and Walter's needs. Over time, this approach can lead to fewer interruptions leading to greater productivity for all.

Disclaimer: This is written for the independent operator who is a kind benevolent dictator and may not be well-suited for someone in the corporate world depending on your company policies.

However, anyone working under the condition of an open-door policy, will suffer from lack of productivity. Individuals tend to abuse this often. If this is your situation, just make sure you look incredibly busy even if you're not. Maybe they will get the hint and bother some other unsuspecting victim. How you utilize your time is up to you. Just as important is how you allow others to use your time. Consistently enforcing boundaries and redirecting interruptions to designated times can help train colleagues to respect your focus and priorities.

Understanding the importance of time management is crucial at any age. Younger individuals may not fully grasp the significance of time until later in life. Some of you reading this may even be saying, "What's the big deal with the time management issue?" A lot. Let me explain. I was not born at my current age. I was young once and did not think too much about time. I certainly am now, and I encourage you to as well. Reflecting on personal and professional experiences and learning from past mistakes is a valuable part of growth. By sharing insights and lessons learned throughout this book, I hope to help you avoid similar pitfalls and make more informed choices about how to invest your time and energy within your business. I wish someone had pulled me aside and helped me understand the value of time at an early age. No one did. If at any point during my years of formal education there was class dedicated solely to time management, I would have been a better steward of time and treated it as a precious resource. Being mindful of how you allocate time can lead to greater productivity, success, and overall satisfaction in life.

Punctuality

Punctuality is something I pride myself in. It is a fundamental aspect of professionalism and requires self-discipline. Somedays much more than others. Demonstrating punctuality to your staff sets a positive example. It also communicates a strong message about the values and expectations of your business. If you yourself arrive late for work, meetings, appointments with clients, etc., you run the risk of your staff devaluing you, your clients, and ultimately your business. Punctuality is closely linked to overall productivity. The same is true for clients and customers. Prioritize punctuality to foster respect and hold yourself and others accountable for it. It sends a clear message that you are committed to excellence and a person who operates with high values of respect for your time and the time of others.

Time Wasters

Social media platforms are designed using algorithms to keep users engaged as long as possible. By prioritizing content that generates an interaction, it can be a valuable tool for your business to connect with customers. This can make good business if you can monetize the interaction. I won't dwell on this topic here and encourage you to conduct careful research into this complex system. The point is that it is crucial for business owners and entrepreneurs to avoid potential pitfalls of excessive social media use, particularly meaningless distractions leading to reduced productivity and negative impacts to your own well-being. Yes, I said it. It is best to establish boundaries and allocate time wisely, avoiding excessive consumption of irrelevant or unproductive content or comments. Rather, be proactive and limit your exposure by exercising discipline and moderation so you can prioritize activities that contribute to your success and fulfillment. There is no shortage of "time vampires" waiting for you to react. Remember, time is democratic, and we all have the same twenty-four hours in the day. While these technologies can offer conveniences and connectivity, they can distract us easily and before you realize, you have invested a portion of your valuable time reading some post on how many days until Christmas or being enticed by the countless political memes for one or the other candidate and even becoming an onlooker into the wild world of electronic shouting matches. A great sign of your intentional behavior to take control over your digital habit is already evidenced by the fact that you are reading this book! I will add further that the same holds true for texting. I don't know who invented the cell phone, but it was pure brilliance. Again, establish boundaries and discern where and when to invest your precious time. I have to believe you know what I'm referring to – surely we have all been included in a debate that ensued on a group text. The cell phone buzzes and the concept of Pavlov's Dogs is further cemented – we immediately and reflexively respond. Individuals automatically react to the specific stimulus and is not under conscious control. It's up to you to take control and to become intentional – reclaim your time and don't let any little black box control you.

Pareto's Law

Absolutely, Pareto's Law, or the 20/80 principle, can be applied to time management as well. By identifying the most critical tasks that yield the greatest results, you can prioritize your efforts and maximize productivity. Additionally, you will be well equipped to eliminate or delegate tasks that detract from your overall effectiveness. Be certain to remove those distractions as quickly as possible.

5 MATH

> *"Arithmetic is not an opinion."*
> **Italian Proverb**

At the risk of being redundant, you'll recall the old adage, "cash flow is more important than your mother". Again, no offense to your mom. Cash flow represents the life blood of any business, enabling it to cover expenses, invest in growth opportunities, and ultimately thrive long-term. Therefore, it is critical to become familiar with and gain proficiency with the math behind your business. I would even go so far as to say that before you even open the doors, invest your time in a managerial accounting class to gain valuable insights into cash flow management, budgeting, forecasting and even interpreting financial statements. It would prove to be a very wise investment of your time and well worth the money. The more you know about cash flow and balance sheets, the better you'll be at mitigating financial challenges and positioning your business for sustainable growth and success.

5 MATH

HINT:
Maintain short-term cash accounts in a money-market fund. Money-market accounts offer liquidity, safety, and potentially higher yields. By keeping only necessary funds in checking accounts to cover the monthly expenses, you minimize idle cash so you can maximize your returns.

These are critical components to the success of your business, but there are a few more that are just as important, maybe even more so. Understanding the long-term value (LTV) of a customer is crucial. Influential figures in direct marketing, such as Dan Kennedy, Gary Halbert, and Drayton Bird, emphasize the significance of this metric. Why? Because you can make an accurate assessment of how much you can afford to spend on acquiring new customers, moreover if you can outspend your competition while maintaining profitability in the long run!

I mentioned earlier that we still have customers who have been ordering from us for over thirty years. You'd better believe that I know the revenue generated during that time by this long-term customer base. I would love to go to some secret lab and clone about five hundred more of them! If it was only that easy.

Another good number is the average transaction value (ATV) of a particular customer. This can provide you with invaluable insights into customer spending habits and help you optimize your marketing strategy. We invested in a point of sale (POS) system that does an excellent job of tracking this number as well as identifying our top spending customers. Using this tool allows you to offer personalized incentives to encourage repeat business and loyalty.

By analyzing data on ATV, you can identify opportunities to increase sales. In the restaurant business, it's why the waitress is trying to offer you appetizers (cross-sell), and more expensive wine or a fancy Italian gelato made by blind Jesuit monks (up-sell). You get the picture. It increases the sale which in turn, ideally, increases the tip.

Understanding customer value (CV), is yet another powerful analysis used to optimize your marketing efforts. Why? These numbers allow you to implement strategies to maximize customer relationships and drive sustainable growth. First step to analyzing CV is segmentation. This view allows you to segment your customer base into different categories – for example, an A-B-C list. The "A" list is where the 20/80 comes into play. That is to say that 80% of your sales will come from 20% of your clients. These customers, to borrow a marketing term, are your "fans" and should be recognized as high-value customers. These customers contribute a significant portion to your company's revenue and are more likely to be loyal advocates for your brand. I will address this further in Chapter 7: Marketing.

Moving to the "B" and "C" list groups, understanding their value allows you to build strategies to develop stronger and more meaningful relationships. Using CV analysis, you can identify potential high-value customers to target – for example, customers within the "B" group where a bit more personalized attention, exceptional service, or exclusive offers, can entice them to increase their LTV and foster loyalty. In short, move them from the "B" group to the "A" group. The

"C" group will require yet another strategy altogether. This could include targeting new customers, or implementing tactics to retain those that have diminishing sales. As evident by this discussion, each of these market segments will require a different approach. They will need unique value propositions based on their buying patterns which will be part of your strategy session.

I know that the term "fire" your customer doesn't sound like a revenue-generating tactic. However, not all customers align with your brand's value or offerings and continuing to allocate marketing dollars to them compromises your resources, thereby negatively impacting growth and profitability. Firing these low-value customers allows you to dedicate that capital to acquiring and retaining customers who are more likely to drive sustainable results and is indeed worth your efforts.

Firing customers, or discontinuing business relationships, is indeed a strategic decision aimed at maximizing returns on investment (ROI). I know, I know the customer is always right. When considering this option, you will need to do the math to fully understand the CV to determine if it is more cost-effective to reallocate resources to more profitable areas of the business.

HINT:
Keep an eye on cash flow. A cash flow spreadsheet on a 13-week rolling basis is a prudent idea.

Understanding metrics like cost per lead and cost per sale, are a few other numbers that are crucial for assessing the effectiveness of marketing efforts and optimizing ROI. In fact, Dan Kennedy refers to them as some of the most critical.

These numbers provide you with tangible insights into what it costs to bring in a sales lead all the way through the conversion process progressing to an eventual sale. This depends on the types of media in use, cost per medium, etc. Also worth repeating: what gets measured improves. The nature of your business and the products or services you offer will impact these metrics. For example, selling high-valued private jets will likely involve higher acquisition costs compared to selling lower-cost items like hamburgers. However, the LTV of the customer needs to be considered. If you retain a customer for 40 years and he's buying a new jet every two years, you can estimate what it costs to bring in likeminded clients. Likewise, the same holds true for customers purchasing lower value goods and services and what you're willing to spend on them. This reiterates the importance of understanding ATV. Remember, nothing happens until something gets sold!

I want to take a moment to mention the social media platform again. I know I'm repeating myself here, but it has been said that repetition is the mother of learning, so it is worth the redundancy. These tech wonders are a double-edged sword. These platforms offer brand exposure and it's nice to have likes and followers engaging. However, they don't directly translate into revenue. If I'm not mistaken, you can't pay the rent with a thumbs up – if you can, please let me know the name of your landlord! Your business transacts in dollars as do your employees. I will touch base on this a bit more in Chapter 7: Marketing. From a number's perspective, it is vital to leverage social media to drive meaningful actions and get customers "off the fence", so to speak, and instead to open their wallets by visiting your website or establishment to make a purchase. Direct followers to targeted landing

5 MATH

pages with compelling offers. This simple step can impact your social media presence but more importantly, can ensure they contribute to your bottom line. Furthermore, if you are spending time on social media and not focusing on converting engagement into dollars, you're wasting productive time. MHO... my humble opinion, its drivel. Take caution and don't get lost in vanity metrics. The numbers don't lie.

6 PHILOSOPHIES

> *"You have your way. I have my way. As for the right way, the correct way, and the only way, it does not exist"*
> **Fredrich Nietzsche**

I will be frank here. I don't live with passion every day. Sorry Tony Robbins. Some days my heart just isn't in it. I believe that success leaves clues and thankfully, learning from the experience and insights of others can also be an invaluable part of your own journey. For example, the wheel was invented in 3,500 BC and it works really well, therefore you and I don't need to reinvent it. There are certain mindsets that lead to business success. I think the earlier that you can adopt them the better off you will be. Oftentimes you'll need to get out of your own way of thinking. Our own limiting beliefs or narrow perspectives can hinder our progress. By being open to new ideas and approaches, including learning from the successes and failures of others before us, we not only expand our own thinking but also increase our chances for success. For this very reason, I'm including this chapter.

Firstly, I feel it's an excellent habit to read and read often. Yes, that means actual books and not just relying solely on the internet. Much of what you read may prove to be irrelevant, noise, or just simply useless. Hopefully not this book. When you find insightful nuggets of information, both you and your business will benefit.

A classic book that I highly recommend reading, and even rereading, as well as keeping on your bookshelf as a great reference tool, is the book "Think and Grow Rich" by Napoleon Hill. Here is a bit of background. As a young man, Napoleon Hill was commissioned by Andrew Carnegie to go out and study the most successful men of his time. This was well over a century ago. Over the course of many years, Hill interviewed and studied the most successful men and compiled a list of their most successful habits and traits. Men such as John Rockefeller, Andrew Carnegie, Henry Firestone, and Thomas Edison. What follows are but a few of the habits or traits that these men shared. Despite very humble beginnings, these men rose to become industry titans who literally built this country. For example, Andrew Carnegie came to the United States at the age of 12 with pennies in his pocket. He went on to form what is known today as U S steel. In fact, we can thank Carnegie for the library system that is in the United States today. The substantial endowment of millions of dollars enabled wonderful libraries to be built and enjoyed by American citizens. I will add, however, that it is reported that many of these guys had sharp elbows – that's not the point. The point is that many of them shared the attributes that contributed to their success. You can simply use them to build your own success story. Remember what I said, success does leave a few clues, and here they are courtesy of Napoleon hill.

Hint:
Take a millionaire to lunch and instead of picking your teeth, pick his brain for ideas for success. It's well worth a steak dinner!

While I won't go into all of them for you, we'll look at just a few to give you an idea of how they work. As mentioned earlier, reading the book "Thank and Grow Rich" would greatly benefit both your business and personal life. Let's start with "the habit of saving". This is an important one. There's an old cliché in business that says, "pay yourself first!" When your business starts turning a profit, aim to save at least 10% of your income if you can! I can't emphasize this enough. Set up retirement accounts like a solo 401(K) or Roth IRA. Automate the process to divert the funds into the account or accounts so they seem less available for spending. This is especially true for the younger entrepreneurs out there; time will be on your side. You won't regret it.

Next is "accurate thinking". This will take much resolve on your part, particularly in today's world. Don't confuse information with knowledge. As Mark Twain once said, "It's the difference between lightning and a lightning bug." No one ever said what we need in this world is more information.

We have information coming out of our ears, but what we need is finely tuned critical thinking skills to separate facts from fiction, lies from truth. The term actionable intelligence comes to mind here. One must be quite careful not to let one's opinions cloud important business decisions. This has been the ruin of many organizations, both large and small, all throughout history. One classic example of this is when Napoleon decided to attack Russia. He entered Russia with an army of over 300,000 men. He left with approximately 10,000. What is the moral of this story other than don't attack Russia? Don't let your ego get in the way of facts!

Next is "concentration". This is an important attribute to have these days as well. In the chapter on time management, I alluded to how often someone is interrupted during their workday, making it challenging to stay on task. So, having a laser-like focus on the task at hand is extremely important. Ensure you have quiet time to be productive by clearing your calendar, turning off the phone, shutting the door, locking yourself in a vault if you must, but make sure that you have allocated quiet time to do the important work of concentrating and focusing on your business. You'll be glad you did.

Lastly, "profit by failure". Failure is giving up. That's failure! I encourage you to take a step back, better yet, get out and walk. In that solitude sometimes you can come up with an innovative solution to a problem. The history of business is replete with stories of successful individuals who persisted with the task at hand despite failures, using them as feedback from the universe. So, be persistent. Thomas Edison was once asked if he wanted to give up on the invention of the lightbulb after failing 1,000 times. His reply, *"No, I just know 999 ways it doesn't work."* There is a big distinction between failure and profiting from failure. My suggestion would be to embrace the opportunity to make big mistakes quickly, learn from them, and quickly move forward. I recall watching a documentary on History Channel, The Food That Built America, about the titans of the food industry and how they pushed the envelope of innovation to get start and the stories of the failures along the way. It's worth a watch.

We covered just a few of the concepts of this ideology. However, I highly recommend investigating further to explore other books to keep to build your own reference library. Remember, success leaves clues and patterns. Try to follow them to build your own business success. Here's to it!

7 Marketing

> *"The best marketing of all is happy clients."*
> **Susan Stripling**

This is perhaps the most important chapter in this book. I only wish that someone had told me about this earlier in my career, as it could have saved me much heartache and pain. But isn't that what life is all about – learning? Anyway, you can have the best widget on planet earth, but it's not much use if you don't sell it.

You see, people, customers, civilians, or whatever else you refer to them as, are funny creatures. WIIFM – do you know the meaning of this acronym? "What's In It For Me?" Additionally, it's the radio station most of us are tuned into. Take a moment to wrap your head around that and grasp its meaning fully. In fact, make it a foundational principle and integrate it into your marketing strategy. Even consider posting a sign simply stating WIIFM on your wall so that it becomes so deeply ingrained in your mind that all your marketing will start with that premise! I know, I know, this old world is selfish. That said, it's also the absolute truth. Don't believe me? Test it out at a social gathering. Strike up a conversation with a group and it won't be long before you find that the conversation has revolved around individuals talking about themselves and very likely not listening to you.

Personally, I find self-centered conversations to be boring. But, self-interest is human nature However, you can and should use that understanding to your advantage. The sooner you craft and articulate your unique selling proposition (USP) in a compelling manner to your market, the better. Research marketing ads and you will find many companies talk about themselves. What they miss is the connection to you and why their brand is to be set apart from all the rest. This is a huge mistake and a great deal of marketing dollars are spent doing this very thing. Whereas large companies may have shareholder support and large budgets that can fund this ineffective style of marketing, small businesses won't have the same luxury. Every marketing dollar must be maximized to keep the business thriving!

I previously mentioned that my background is in the restaurant and hospitality industry. However, that's not true. It took a long time to realize that we were in the business of marketing our restaurant's goods and services. That's also the business you're in- marketing your business's goods and services. Don't make the same mistake I did. But again, you're smarter than that. That's why you're reading this book.

Try not to fool yourself about this. If you can't effectively market your enterprise's goods and services, you won't be in business for long. It's a critical skill set. This is wholly counterintuitive. You may say to yourself, "I'm the world's greatest chef. If I build it, they will come." That's a parochial idea at best. I used to think that as well, until experience taught me otherwise. For example, 60% of restaurants fail within

7 MARKETING

the first three years of operation*. You may indeed be the best at what you do. But if you can't convey that value or benefit through a carefully crafted marketing message, targeted to the right market using the right medium, you'll face challenges.

*Source: Ohio State University Study

However, don't despair. The good news is that you don't have to be the best! Improving your marketing skills will be crucial. You see, you can be a big fish in a small pond and excel in a smaller market space. Like that old saying goes, "In the land of the blind, the one-eyed man is king." Be honest with yourself here and reflect on this: would you prefer closing your business, thinking you were the best, or witness consistent growth in your cash flow and bank account year after year? I trust you chose the former over the latter.

Ego can cloud prudent business decisions. This is a lesson I've learned firsthand from brutal experiences. Guard yourself against this pitfall. Check your ego at the door and prioritize facts over opinions. And trust me on this, everyone will have one. You will have to have the wisdom of Solomon to discern the right path. Avoid being swayed by grand schemes that you see on social media platforms or TV reality shows; they're not reflective of reality. So do yourself a favor and instead, read books to educate yourself. You'll be glad you did!

There is an old saying that you would do well to remember, "Rich people have big libraries, poor people have big TVs." Reaching that level of wealth is seeming rare, this book is not about that. I'm not saying you shouldn't pursue excellence – you should go for it! I'm saying you should be aware of and prepared for roadblocks on the road to success.

At a fundamental level, you need to develop marketing systems, Particularly direct response marketing systems that promote your product or service. I emphasize direct response marketing for a reason: it can be measured. You'll recall I mentioned this twice before that what gets measured improves. I will be the first to admit I'm not the most tech savvy guy in the world. Heck, I still have a rotary phone – I'm kidding, of course! My point is I'm not a technophobe either so these fundamental marketing tactics are achievable regardless of your skill level.

HINT: Refer to Chapter 2: Systems!

Social media can have a place in your marketing strategy if, and that's a BIG IF, it's held accountable. Personally, I'm not on Facebook and never will be because I see it as a significant time drain. However, our business does have social media sites. I'm told by those that oversee these pages that we have a certain number of likes. Now my ego says, "Oh, that's great, people like us." My marketing mind, the one that pays the bills says, "Will I be able to make payroll every two weeks with this amount of likes?" The short answer is no, and neither will you.

You'll recall the discussion earlier when I touched on social media. The fact remains the same in this chapter: you and I get paid in dollars not likes – perhaps one day in cryptocurrency or seashells or maybe even likes, but for now, little pieces of paper with dead presidents' pictures on them. Dollars. Your mission, should you choose to accept it, is clear: move these individuals off the fence e and monetize social media. Transition them from merely liking you by giving

7 MARKETING

you a thumbs up or even a heart to opening their wallets and making a purchase from you.

Direct them to a landing or your website with an enticing offer! Encourage them to take action and provide you with their contact information and perhaps even some additional information such as birthdate. Once you are successful with capturing that information and them to your database, you will then have the ability to upsell to them. The goal is to convert them into lifelong customers. Remember the value of a lifelong customer? Refer to Chapter 5: Match as a reminder. Knowing the value of a lifelong customer allows you to determine how much you can invest in acquiring them. That is the most important reason to have social media. In short, if it isn't contributing to your bottom line, it is crucial that you ensure that it does.

Without question, accountability is paramount, especially when it comes to marketing. It must make sense, hopefully dollar$ and cent$! With a direct response marketing system, you will be able to track and measure the effectiveness of your efforts and have that accountability. For example, I know that when I promote an offer to a select customer base, there is a certain return. While it is not always the same, there is an average. The goal of this strategy is not only to generate revenue, but also to ensure a profit. These social media platforms also need to be leveraged to drive revenue and customer engagement. Ultimately, as a business owner, your focus should be on converting leads into paying customers and maximizing the return on your marketing investment. Remember, you're in the marketing business now!

Without question, the content on social media can vary widely in quality and relevance. From a business perspective, it's essential to leverage social media platforms to drive traffic to your website or landing page, where you can convert leads into sales. Additionally, there is no shortage of sales reps from any number of advertising and promotional sites calling to tell you what your business needs – the latest and greatest digital and print marketing scheme delivering more words than profit. Most of this is costly fluff. What truly matters for your business is attracting customers genuinely value your products or services and are willing to refer others to your business.

I can hear your argument now, "you're old and this is the new way." You are correct, I am older today than I was yesterday. But while the medium may evolve, human nature remains fundamentally unchanged. Emotions like lust, fear, desperation, and greed continue to drive human behavior, regardless of technological advancements. As old as murder may be, it still occurs today, highlighting the enduring aspects of human nature. So, while the methods of communication may shift, the underlying motivations and responses of humanity remain constant.

You would do well to keep that in mind when it comes to your marketing strategies. While embracing new technologies and platforms, it is essential to ensure accountability. For example, the strategy generates tangible results, and can be proven by the contributions to the bottom line. Don't discard the fundamentals of marketing for the allure of the next new shiny object; instead integrate new approaches while you stay firmly grounded in practices that drive success.

For these reasons, I am a big fan of cultivating and leveraging your house list or your database of customers as a powerful strategy. When customers willingly opt in

7 MARKETING

or engage with your business via a landing page, coupon or good old-fashioned pencil and paper, they're expressing interest and familiarity that signals their readiness to engage further. They're raising their hands and saying, "Me too!" They know about your business or your product. Or perhaps they were in your brick-and-mortar establishment. Ah yes, buildings – they do still exist and can entice clientele to enter. Why do I digress? Because we are still human after all, and we need one another and business establishments can be warm, inviting gathering places. Ensuring that your place of business is clean, inviting, and clearly communicates your operations, products, and services is another great way of attracting and retaining customers. Let's get back to the topic. To maintain customer engagement and loyalty, you need to build rapport through regular contact. Charm them if you will. Keep in constant contact but you don't always have to sell them. Sharing genuine communications such as stories about your business or updates happening, help to strengthen the connection with customers making them much more likely to choose you over competitors where there is little rapport or familiarity.

FACT: Acquiring a new client requires six times the effort compared to selling to an existing one.

Largely, the goal of being in business is to achieve financial success. Isn't that what you're in business for – to try and get rich or improve your financial position? If your customers can't contribute to that, who will? Be warned however, this is an ongoing battle for the loyalty, hearts and minds of your guests, clients, patients, etc. This is no easy task and requires diligent effort and handled as a top priority. It's hard work, but remember, work smarter, not harder.

Direct response marketing is the area of your business that demands laser-like focus. Even if you're juggling multiple responsibilities, prioritize this and delegate tasks if need be. I realize that is not easy, especially if you are just getting started or are a sole proprietor. As an entrepreneur, and driving force behind your business, you need to wear many hats. The hat of marketing, in particular direct response marketing, is essential for sustaining profitability and growth – and that is what keeps the bills paid and the lights on.

I mentioned earlier that I wished someone would have given me this advice long ago. It certainly would have saved quite a bit of work, and sweat, had we developed marketing systems at the onset. I have met entrepreneurs who, upon starting their businesses, immediately invested in t-shirts and business cards proclaiming themselves as the company president. That's all well and good and seemingly impressive, although their tenure was short-lived. Within six months to a year, many of these businesses failed.

With that said, before you sign a lease, create a cool website, or have t-shirts made, go to school! That doesn't mean go out and get an MBA. This stuff is not theory. By going to school, I mean take at least six months, if not more, and study direct response marketing systems. Include this as a vital part of your overall planning. It will be money and time well spent. Explore books and influential marketing professionals mentioned here, and delve into marketing websites, blogs, and podcasts to get yourself familiar with concepts. Marketing is one component of many within the systems of your enterprise.

7 MARKETING

But again, as I said, it is the most important. You should take the helm and lead your business to success. Treat it like your child: nurture it, feed it, and watch it grow. You'll be thankful you did. Now let's look at some marketing numbers.

These are some statistics that might surprise you. Keeping in mind that much of this material, in particular marketing, is rather counterintuitive, blending science and art. Here are some reasons why people do business with you.

1. Confidence
2. Quality
3. Service
4. Selection
5. Price

Take notice of the disparity between the top and bottom reasons. In the number one slot is confidence. Here are some important questions to ask yourself about your business: 1) Do your customers have confidence that you will fulfill your promise and deliver on time? 2) Will you meet their expectations? 3) Why is confidence more important than price alone? 4) Do you really want a customer or client who prioritizes only the cheapest option?

Price is a relative concept and there is such a concept known as price elasticity. If your business relies solely on offering the lowest price, you need significant economies of scale to sustain it. You will be playing a losing game against big box competitors. With greater profitability, you are equipped to invest more to out-market the competition and promote your unique selling proposition. It's better to be a big fish in a small pond.

Here are a few more numbers that should be of profound interest to you and your business. The attrition factor: why businesses lose customers.

1. 1% die
2. 3% move away
3. 5% follow friends and switch
4. 9% switch for price/better product
5. 14% product dissatisfaction
6. 68% leave because of INDIFFERENCE, FEELING UNAPPRECIATED, AND UNIMPORTANT!

Let's dissect further. There is not much you can do about number one. It is a truism of life itself. Therefore, we will not dwell on it. The second point, people relocating, is yet another fact of life and not much you can do about that either. People move for several reasons, job, retirement, etc. However, with advances in technology that have diminished barriers of trade, you can still sell to those who have moved, depending on what you sell.

Approximately 5 percent of individuals will follow a friend's advice and chose to go to a competitor. At number four, approximately 9 percent will switch for a better price. This could actually work in your favor. More on that later. So, approximately 18 percent of customers will disappear due to attrition. Therefore, it's so important to keep them for as long as you possibly can. Additionally, implementing a lead generation program is essential to replenish the customer base.

Now for the good news! The remaining 82 percent are within your control to influence! And you should! Let's focus on the number four reason: about 9 percent will leave for price.

7 MARKETING

I mentioned that this may be to your benefit. The reason is that they are in essence "firing" themselves sparing you the effort. Recognizing you can't be all things to all people, you can reallocate your marketing dollars spent on these clients to attract more suitable customers that more favorably align with your business.

Unless you have economies of scale that drive down your costs and attain sufficient market share necessary, it's imperative to set prices that cover expenses and generates profit. That profit allows you the ability to target your marketing efforts to customers willing to pay the prices you've set.

Coming in at number four: 14 percent will leave for product satisfaction. We don't need to dwell on ethics too much here. I am going to assume that you have a quality product, and that you are a decent human being, not intending anyone harm. With that said, having a 100% MONEY BACK GUARANTEE is a must! Recall from earlier in the chapter that the number one reason people do business with you is confidence! They want assurance that you will be there if something goes wrong, and that you stand behind it. A solid guarantee does just that. It's now even more important given the times in which we live.

Now the biggest reason why people stop doing business with you – drum roll please... INDIFFERENCE, FEELING UNAPPRECIATED, AND UNIMPORTANT! I emphasize these points because they are entirely within your control to address and mitigate, and you should. Having a well-maintained customer database that is routinely updated is an excellent way to do this.

Consider tactics like sending out birthday and anniversary offers and a variety of other value propositions that will make them feel special. Of course, you don't always have to give them something for free; as mentioned, sharing a story or providing helpful insights for their benefit is also a great option. The key is that the more ways you communicate with them, the better. And do it often!

And including a call to action is always a good idea. This is the next step that you desire for them to take and is strategically placed to prompt an immediate response. For example, "sign up today."

8 Crisis Management

> "When written in Chinese, the word 'crisis' is composed of two characters. One represents danger, the other opportunity."
> **John F. Kennedy**

JFK was famous for saying many witty things and one of my favorites was when he told the incoming Secretary of Defense, Bob McNamara, *"There's no manual for being the president either Bob."* There certainly isn't one for being a human either. What I'm going to do is provide you with one. Please keep in mind that as of the time that this was written, a crisis was well underway. When a crisis occurs, generally the first response to kick in is fear – real human fear. Make no mistake about this. It's that important not to underestimate this.

You can expect pundits and preachers quoting famous figures on why not to fear. That's nonsense! You're going to be afraid – it's inevitable. I know I was, and there's nothing wrong with that. In fact, it's completely natural. Congratulations you're a human being. For me, the key was not to dwell on that fear. 2020 was like no other time for most living humans. We often think such things won't, or can't happen to us, but they certainly can and most surely did. What followed was one of the most surreal years anyone could have imagined. It is my sincere hope that it's going to be the last in our lifetimes. 2020 presented unique challenges, personally and professionally, that we all had to face. While far from enjoyable, we had to confront it nonetheless and under difficult circumstances.

As this is a book about business, I will try to keep it concise and to that point. In the initial stages of this crisis, panic set in on many fronts. As the shutdown began, people scrambled for the basic supplies and even had fist-fights over toilet paper. From my experience, it's wise to acknowledge any fears that you have, then set them aside and focus on the facts available. Given the limited information from any government officials, you'll need to rely on your own judgment.

Quite frankly, I'm genuinely surprised at how quickly certain branches of our government responded to the crisis. Their inconsistency to accomplish this on an ongoing basis is beyond my comprehension. It is essential that you focus on the things that you can control and tune out the rest of the noise. From a business perspective, I recommend focusing on your cashflow situation with the utmost precision. This is the most, or one of the most, important things during the best of days and circumstances. It is most certainly mission critical in the time of a crisis. Take a thorough inventory of your cash flow situation.

For example, meticulously track your cash on hand that you have in the bank accounts and monitor it closely. Consider setting up a weekly spreadsheet to oversee your cashflow situation to keep track of expenses. Depending on your circumstances, I would recommend conducting weekly, if not daily, reviews. Your labor costs, one of your largest expenses,

8 CRISIS MANAGEMENT

should also be closely monitored. You may have to get creative or make tough decisions, such as reducing hours or laying off employees. Reducing hours or staff during close times should be done on a regular basis. In a crisis, you may have no other choice but to do so. While fear may creep in and potentially paralyze you, it's crucial to confront these challenges head-on.

During times like these, you're going to need to maintain an unwavering focus on the facts and take decision action as appropriate. The viability of your enterprise will depend on it. Consider this: if your business were to fail during favorable conditions, what would stakeholders care about most? Likely, very few would know or perhaps even care. If you are eligible for assistance from any governmental agency, as was the case during this pandemic, take advantage of the opportunity and do it immediately. Don't let pride jeopardize the survival of your business. Even if it means obtaining an interest-free loan that requires repayment, utilize them to stabilize your business until conditions improve.

It goes without saying that if you can obtain a grant that doesn't require repayment, that's the preferrable option, especially during a time of crises. As I mentioned, cash flow is paramount in time of crisis, as it may take months, if not years, to fully recover. I would also recommend reaching out to your vendors negotiate extended credit terms or better payment options. While there's a chance that they will not be able to accommodate your request due to their own cash flow constraints, it's still worth pursuing to safeguard your business's survival.

In conclusion, my sincere hope is that this book can prove to be helpful to you. I wish all of you business owners and aspiring entrepreneurs the best of luck in your endeavors!

ABOUT THE AUTHOR

Stephan Daniels has lived and worked in the Midwest his entire life and has real world experiences in an entrepreneurial setting.

Acclaim for the book.

> "The book is filled with real-world experiences and practical tips that any business owner can put into practice." Mark Toohey, Property Manager, Hawaii

> "I love the way Steve puts a personal touch on managing his family-owned business, it shows…" Dave Krahn, GOP Treasurer, Kendall County, Il

> "I've known Steve for some time now, and his is the type of knowledge that gets results, ignore at your own peril." Phil Nelson, President Nelson Inc.

www.ingramcontent.com/pod-product-compliance
Lightning Source LLC
Chambersburg PA
CBHW031548210526
45464CB00003B/1201